Creatures All Around Us
Sea Snakes

by D. M. Souza

🌿 **Carolrhoda Books, Inc./Minneapolis**

The publisher wishes to thank Dr. Harold Heatwole, Head of the Department of Zoology, North Carolina State University for his help in the preparation of this book.

Carolrhoda Books, Inc., c/o The Lerner Publishing Group
241 First Avenue North, Minneapolis, MN 55401 U.S.A.

Website address: www.lernerbooks.com

Library of Congress Cataloging-in-Publication Data

Souza, D. M. (Dorothy M.)
     Sea snakes / by D. M. Souza.
         p.   cm.—(Creatures all around us)
     Includes index.
     Summary: Describes the physical characteristics, habits, habitats, and life cycle of sea snakes.
     ISBN 1-57505-263-6 (alk. paper)
     1. Sea snakes—Juvenile literature. [1. Sea snakes. 2. Snakes.]
I. Title. II. Series: Souza, D. M. (Dorothy M.). Creatures all around us.
QL666.O645S68 1998
597.96'177—dc21   97-17996

Manufactured in the United States of America
1 2 3 4 5 6 – JR – 03 02 01 00 99 98

A true sea snake rests on the ocean floor.

Deadly Snakes in the Sea

A snake's thick, olive-colored body is coiled on the seafloor beneath a forest of corals. The lidless eyes on either side of its small, pointed head are open—yet the snake is asleep. It's been asleep for almost an hour.

Nearby, a similar-looking snake slips its tongue in and out of its mouth, trying to catch the scent of food. Its body is long and graceful. No one would guess that these two creatures are among the deadliest of all snakes. Both are true sea snakes, members of the Hydrophiidae (hy-DROF-ih-dee) family.

This red-sided garter snake spends part of its time in lakes and streams. But, unlike true sea snakes, it also spends time on land.

Many snakes, such as water and garter snakes, swim in lakes, pools, and streams. Other snakes hunt for food in salty marshes and coastal waters. But all of these swimming snakes also spend some time on land. Only true sea snakes live their entire lives in water. About 50 different species (SPEE-sheez), or kinds, of true sea snakes can be found in the warm parts of the Indian and Pacific Oceans.

Some scientists believe that true sea snakes once belonged to the same family as the cobra—a **terrestrial** (teh-REHS-tree-uhl), or land-dwelling, variety of snake. Other scientists believe that sea snakes came from an ancient family of water snakes that no longer exists. Still other scientists think it's possible that about 25 to 30 million years ago, some land snakes began to search for food in the sea. Gradually they spent more and more time in the water, until finally they stopped returning to land altogether. These snakes may have developed into true sea snakes.

The cobra is a terrestrial snake. Some scientists think true sea snakes came from the cobra family.

Sea snakes are reptiles. Like other reptiles, they have backbones, breathe air, and are **ectothermic** (ek-tuh-THUR-mik), meaning their body temperature changes with the temperature of their surroundings. They are also covered with two layers of skin. The inner layer of skin, called the dermis (DUR-mis), is soft and stretchy, while the outer one, called the epidermis (ep-uh-DUR-mis), is leathery and scaly.

The scales of sea snakes may be smooth, rough, or as bumpy as the kernels on an ear of corn. Some have **keels,** or ridges, down the middle of each scale. Tight-fitting scales allow them to move smoothly through the water.

A sea snake's outer skin is leathery, with tight-fitting scales.

This yellow-bellied sea snake struggles to get back into the ocean. Its belly scales are not made for crawling on land.

Land snakes have large, tough scales on their bellies that help them grip the ground when they move. Sea snakes have belly scales that are small and smooth. If a storm washes a sea snake up onto a beach, it cannot easily crawl back into the water by itself. Instead, it must wait for an incoming wave to carry it out to sea again. If a wave does not reach the sea snake and it becomes stranded under the sizzling rays of the sun, the sea snake soon dies.

In the sea, however, sea snakes move with ease. The reptiles have several hundred vertebrae (VURT-uh-bray), or short sections of backbone, that are moveable. When the snakes begin to swim, powerful muscles twist these vertebrae, making their bodies wriggle like the letter S. Then their narrow heads cut through the water and their long, flat tails, like the paddle of a boat, move them silently forward.

When this true sea snake swims through the water, its body looks like the letter S.

Sea snakes, like this one, often live near rocks and coral reefs.

Some sea snakes, such as yellow-bellies, are often found swimming far from land. But most sea snakes stay in shallow coastal waters where they find fish, eels, and eggs to eat. Some sea snakes' **habitats**—or places where they live and hide—are rock crevices, the tangled roots of trees, or coral reefs. Only one kind of sea snake, the *Hydrophis semperi* (hy-DRAH-fis semp-EE-ree), does not live in salt water. It was discovered in a freshwater lake in the Philippine Islands. Scientists believe this sea snake was trapped there long ago when land closed off the entrance to what was once a bay of the sea.

Most sea snakes are between 3 and 5 feet long, but a few have been found that reach over 8 feet. Each of them is specially designed to live underwater, even though they must all have air to breathe.

Long Lungs

This sea snake comes to the surface of the water for a quick breath of air.

The head of a sea snake pokes above the surface of the water for a few seconds to catch some air through two nostrils on the top of its head. After several quick breaths, it disappears. Down, down it dives—30 or more feet beneath the surface.

As the snake descends, several of its body parts go into action. Tissues of skin cover its nostrils so that water cannot enter. Close-fitting scales keep its mouth watertight. Like the snake's land relative's eyes, each of its eyes is covered by a thin, clear **spectacle** (SPEK-tuh-kuhl), or type of scale. Underwater, these spectacles act like a pair of swimming goggles and keep out tiny floating objects.

Sea snakes have a clear scale that covers each of the eyes.

How long can you hold your breath underwater? A sea snake that is hunting or trying to escape an enemy needs a lot of oxygen and will come up for air after 15 or 20 minutes. If it's resting, however, it needs only a little oxygen and can stay underwater for almost two hours! How does it do this?

The lung of the sea snake is almost as long as its body. When this reptile catches a breath of air at the surface, some of the air is stored in a sac at the bottom of the snake's lung. This sac, which also helps the snake float, acts like scuba gear by slowly supplying the animal with air while it's underwater.

When a sea snake is resting, like this one, it can stay underwater for almost two hours before coming up for air.

A sea snake spits out extra salt that has collected under its tongue.

Too much salt can kill any animal. How does the sea snake keep from getting too much salt inside its body, especially when it eats underwater in its salty seawater home? The sea snake has a special structure called a gland under its tongue. This gland—the **sublingual** (suhb-LIHN-gwehl) **gland**—collects extra salt. When the gland becomes full, the snake flicks out its forked tongue and spits out the extra salt.

Fangs

A Dubois's sea snake keeps watch for a tasty meal to come its way.

A Dubois's sea snake nudges its pointed snout into an opening between two rocks. A small eel brushes past it, and the snake strikes swiftly. Two short, needle-sharp **fangs,** or teeth, in the snake's upper jaw prick the eel's body. **Venom** (VEH-nuhm), or poison, from glands on each side of the snake's head, flows through the fangs and into its victim. In minutes the eel is paralyzed—unable to move. The snake begins to swallow the eel, even though it may not be dead yet.

The sea snake's fangs are hollow, like a tube. They are hidden by flesh in the reptile's upper jaw. A second set of fangs usually lies beneath the first and takes over if the first set breaks or falls out. The other teeth in the snake's mouth are solid and do not hold venom.

Sea snakes are **carnivores** (KAR-nuh-vorz), or meat eaters. They feast mainly on fish and eels. Because the waters where they live and hunt are dark, sea snakes do not depend on their eyes to find food to eat. Instead, like land snakes, they use their tongues to pick up the scent of **prey,** or the animals they eat. They also use their sense of touch to feel their prey's movements in the water around them.

This sea snake enjoys a meal.

True sea snakes are carnivores. They enjoy foods like the stone scorpionfish (top) and the ribbon eel (bottom).

Beaked sea snakes swim just above the ocean bottom. Eels and fish are their favorite foods, and they hunt like the Dubois's snake. When a fish brushes past a beaked sea snake, the snake swings its head rapidly sideways, opens its mouth, and sinks its fangs into its catch. Beaked sea snakes hold the fish between their teeth until the venom takes effect and their victim stops struggling. Then they swallow it headfirst.

Many fish that sea snakes catch have sharp spines in their fins. These spines go down more easily if the snake swallows the fish headfirst rather than tailfirst. Once in a while, however, a snake will be spotted with a few spines sticking out of its sides—a sign that it ate its meal the wrong way.

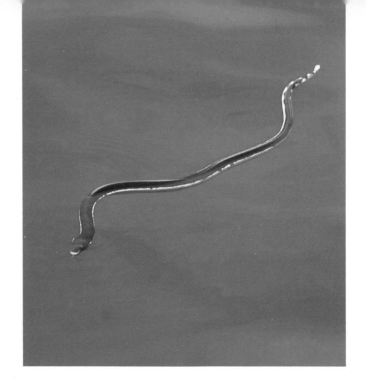

This yellow-bellied sea snake hunts for food near the surface of the water.

Yellow-bellied sea snakes use trickery to catch their food. Often they drift far from land, close to the surface of the water. **Schools,** or groups, of small fish often mistake the snakes' long yellow-and-black bodies for pieces of floating seaweed and swim beneath them for protection. When the yellow-belly feels several fish brush against its tail, it begins to swim backward. As soon as a fish appears near its head, the snake strikes sideways. Its fangs prick the creature, and in minutes, a limp body slips down the snake's throat, headfirst.

A few sea snakes, such as turtle-headed sea snakes, eat mainly fish eggs and do not use their fangs to catch prey. They do have venom, however, and will use it to protect themselves against enemies.

Some sea snakes, like the turtle-headed (below right), bury their heads in the sand to search for fish eggs (below).

In waters surrounding Australia and some Pacific islands, people have to be on the lookout for sea snakes. Swimmers are sometimes bitten when they enter shallow water and do not watch where they are stepping. The bite, which is described as feeling like a pinprick, can be deadly if the person is not treated right away.

Some sea snakes are more dangerous than others. A beaked sea snake's venom is four times more deadly than a cobra's. A single beaked sea snake may carry enough poison to kill 53 people!

A sea snake may bite if a swimmer steps on it.

Baby Snakes

This yellow-bellied sea snake will join hundreds of other yellow-bellies to pair off and mate.

Off the coast of Panama, hundreds of yellow-bellied snakes have come together. The snakes pair off, twisting and turning their bodies around each other beneath the surface of the water. They look as if they are doing a strange dance, but they are actually mating.

During mating, male sea snakes release **sperm,** or male cells, inside the females' bodies. Some of those sperm join with the females' eggs. Then the females move closer to shore, where they float near the surface with their heads and tails hanging down. Slowly the fertilized eggs grow into **embryos** (EM-bree-ohz), or young in the beginning stages of development.

Many female land snakes lay eggs and hide them in warm, safe places under leaves, sand, or logs. After a time, baby snakes break out of the leathery shells and begin to move on their own. Snakes that give birth in this way are called **oviparous** (oh-VIP-uh-ruhs).

Yellow-bellies, however, like all sea snakes and some of their terrestrial relatives, do not lay eggs. Instead, the females keep their developing young inside their bodies in a clear case, called a chorion (KOR-ee-ahn). When it's time to be born, the cases break and the live young slip out of their mother's body. Snakes that give birth in this way are called **viviparous** (vih-VIP-uh-ruhs).

The female yellow-bellies grow larger and heavier before their young are born. The females are unable to swim as quickly as they once did, and they spend much of their time floating near the surface. During the day, they let their bodies, and the young inside them, soak up the warmth of the sun.

As the day of birth draws near, each mother searches for a protected place close to shore that is teeming with small fish. As soon as the young enter their new world, they must take care of themselves, so mothers try to make certain enough food will be nearby.

While most female sea snakes have from 2 to 20 young, yellow-bellies have an average of 4. Each is about 12 inches long.

When the yellow-bellied sea snake is large and heavy from carrying young inside of her, she spends most of her time near the surface.

This sea snake is ready to shed its skin—its eyes are dull and cloudy.

All baby snakes grow quickly and their skins, or coats, soon become too tight—the way your clothes sometimes become too small for you. To solve this problem, snakes **molt,** or shed their coats. Both baby and adult sea snakes molt often—every two to six weeks. Molting not only makes way for a shiny new skin, but also helps sea snakes get rid of tiny creatures that live on them, the way fleas and ticks can live on cats and dogs.

A discarded sea snake skin settles at the bottom of the ocean.

A few weeks before a sea snake molts, an oily liquid forms between its old and new coat and beneath the scale covering each eye. The eyes become dull and cloudy. It doesn't eat, and it snaps when other creatures come near. Gradually, however, its eyes clear. Some sea snakes will then begin to rub their lips against pieces of coral or other hard objects to loosen their old skin. Once the skin around the head breaks, the snake easily crawls out of its old covering and leaves it inside out and in one piece. Then the old skin drifts to the bottom of the ocean, where other creatures snack on it.

Yellow-bellies have a different way of molting, however. When it's time for yellow-bellies to change coats, they tie themselves in knots. They rub the coils of their bodies against themselves until their skins loosen and they can crawl out of them.

It takes about a year for most sea snakes to become adults and look for mates of their own. They may live for three or four years and raise a new family with a new mate each year. Others, such as olive snakes, mate every other year and may live as long as ten years.

These turtle-headed sea snakes are ready to mate.

Fearless

This turtle-headed sea snake steals eggs from a damselfish. Sea snakes have very few enemies.

A turtle-headed sea snake swims along the ocean bottom. Every now and then, it sticks its head into the sand to search for fish eggs. When it finds a large number of eggs, the turtle-headed sea snake buries its head and lets its body and tail sway in the water like a magician's rope. For almost 30 minutes, the snake remains in this position as it eats the eggs. Although there are large, hungry fish swimming around the snake during this time, the sea snake has nothing to fear.

Because of their poisonous fangs, sea snakes have few **predators** (PREH-duh-turz), or other animals that attack and eat them. Sometimes a fish will make the mistake of trying to swallow a sea snake. A few minutes later the fish will cough up its meal. The snake escapes, but the fish often dies from a bite it has received inside its body. Most fish learn to stay away from sea snakes.

A sea snake has caught a fish to eat. If a fish tries to eat a sea snake, the sea snake will give it a deadly bite.

Occasionally, sharks and large moray eels will attack some sea snakes like the Stokes's snake and the beaked snake. But only sea eagles regularly feed on many varieties of sea snakes. They swoop down and grab the reptiles when they come up to the surface to breathe. The eagles then carry the snakes close to shore and kill them by dropping them onto rocks. Dead sea snakes are much less dangerous to eat than live ones!

Most of the time though, sea snakes do not have to hurry or hide when they move in their underwater world. Their deadly fangs are a good weapon against almost any creature who comes near.

This sea eagle has caught a delicious fish to eat. Sea eagles also eat dead sea snakes.

Lookalikes

A sea krait swims near a coral reef.

A 6-foot-long snake cuts through the water with its black-and-yellow head. As it swims, the snake's round, bluish gray body, circled by 40 to 50 black rings, swings from side to side in a series of S movements. The snake pushes against the water and moves forward with its paddlelike tail. This long reptile is a banded sea krait, one of several highly poisonous snakes that are often mistaken for true sea snakes.

A sea krait hunts for food near rocks on the ocean floor.

Four different species of sea kraits, from the family Laticaudidae (lah-tih-KAW-dih-dee), live in many of the same places that sea snakes do. While they are alike in several ways, they are also different.

As the banded sea krait swims underwater, it flicks its tongue in and out of its mouth several times. Suddenly its tongue catches the scent of an eel. When the fish appears from behind a rock, the sea krait swings its head sideways and strikes. Its fangs pierce its victim's body and flood it with venom. In minutes, the eel is paralyzed and the snake begins to swallow it headfirst—dead or alive.

32

After the eel disappears down its throat, the sea krait wriggles its body toward the surface and takes in a breath of air through nostrils on the side of its head. Then it dives under again and swims to shore.

Once on the beach, the sea krait—unlike true sea snakes—begins to crawl on the land. The broad scales on the sea krait's belly push against the ground and move the snake toward a pile of rocks. Here the sea krait rests while it digests its meal. During the day it either suns itself or hides—under rocks or inside a nearby cave.

Sea kraits, unlike true sea snakes, spend part of their time on land. This banded sea krait rests on a pile of rocks.

Thousands of sea kraits often crowd together on tropical islands to mate. Males and females curl their bodies around one another the way other snakes do. After mating, females lay 4 to 20 long, tube-shaped eggs and hide them between rocks, under fallen palm leaves, or in other safe places. Depending on the species of sea krait, some mothers wrap their bodies around the soft-shelled eggs to protect them. Other species leave and never return to guard their eggs.

After they break out of their shells, the 7-inch-long kraits crawl to the ocean and begin to search for food. Most stay close to shore and grow quickly, especially during the first year of their lives.

Sea kraits gather together on tropical islands to mate.

Large numbers of true sea snakes and sea kraits are killed for their skins. Here, a worker makes shoes from sea snake skins.

Although the venom of sea kraits is deadly, the snakes are usually shy around people and will try to escape rather than bite. Sea kraits are especially easy to catch when they come ashore, which is when they are often captured.

Each year large numbers of true sea snakes and their lookalikes, the sea kraits, are killed for their skins. Snake skins are made into belts, wallets, and other items of clothing. In some countries, snake meat is smoked, canned, or sold to restaurants. Leftovers are turned into animal feed, and the fat from the snakes is made into margarines and butters.

Scientists are concerned that sea snakes and sea kraits are being overhunted and are at risk of becoming endangered. The snakes' venom holds many clues about the way human muscles and nerves work. If the reptiles disappear, medical researchers will be unable to discover other important information that may be hidden inside these snakes.

Whether floating on the surface, diving underwater, or moving in and around rocks or coral reefs, sea snakes and their lookalikes are fascinating reptiles. People must do all they can to make certain that these snakes are protected. Then other people will be able to observe and make new discoveries about these unusual reptiles for years to come.

Several different families of snakes have members that spend some of their time in the sea or in freshwater streams, swamps, or marshes, while the rest of their time is spent on land. Only snakes in the Hydrophiidae family live in the sea all the time. They are called true sea snakes and give birth to live young.

Sea kraits are closely related to true sea snakes. Some scientists place them in the same family. Other scientists put sea kraits in a family of their own—the Laticaudidae. Sea kraits leave the water to sun themselves on beaches and lay their eggs in protected places. Below are some members of both of these families and a few facts about each.

FAMILY	EXAMPLES	SIZE IN INCHES	FAVORITE FOODS	HABITAT
Hydrophiidae (sea snakes)	beaked	62	fish, eels	coastal waters
	Dubois's	30-36	fish	coral reefs
	Stokes's	60-78	fish	deep water
	turtle-headed	30	fish eggs	coral reefs
	yellow-bellied	30	fish	coastal waters, open sea
Laticaudidae (sea kraits)	banded	53	fish, eels	coral reefs, mangrove swamps
	black-banded	38	fish, eels	coastal waters, swamps
	yellow-lipped	24-43	eels	mangrove swamps, coastal waters

Glossary

carnivores: animals that eat meat

ectothermic: having a body temperature that changes with the temperature of the environment

embryo: the young of an animal in the beginning stages of its development, before birth

fangs: the hollow teeth of poisonous snakes

habitats: the places where animals live and hide

keels: the ridges found on some scales

molt: to shed skin

oviparous: giving birth by laying eggs that later hatch

predator: an animal that attacks and eats other animals

prey: an animal that is killed and eaten by other animals

schools: large groups of sea creatures, such as fish, that swim together

spectacle: a clear scale that covers each eye of a snake

sperm: the cells of a male animal that fertilize the eggs of a female

sublingual gland: a gland under a snake's tongue that helps it to get rid of extra salt in its blood

terrestrial: growing or living on land

venom: poison

viviparous: giving birth to live young

39

Index